20 lessons

Practical Psychology

To improve your life
and achieve success

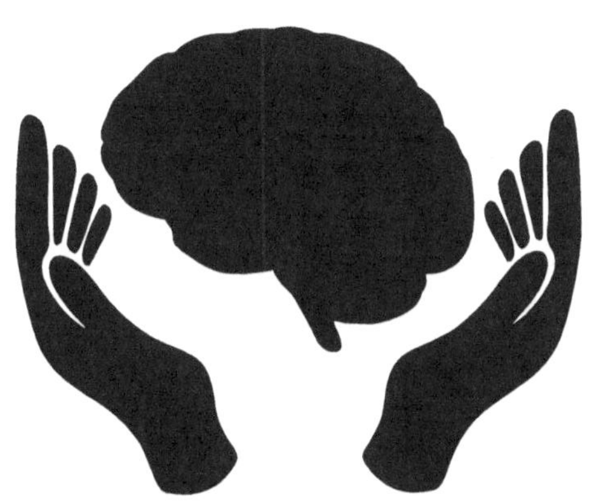

Phillips Tahuer

Ediciones Afrodita

Contents:

Introduction

In a constantly changing world full of challenges, the pursuit of success and personal well-being has become a priority for many people. However, we often find ourselves trapped in patterns of thinking and behavior that prevent us from achieving our goals and living the life we want. This is where psychology, as the science of human behavior, becomes a powerful and transformative tool.

Practical psychology focuses on applying psychological theories and findings to real-world situations. Unlike other, more theoretical streams, which may focus on abstract research and the elaboration of complex conceptual models, practical psychology seeks tangible and effective solutions to the challenges we face in our daily lives. This branch of psychology emphasizes the importance of understanding how to apply psychological knowledge in everyday contexts, providing concrete strategies that people can use to improve their well-being and achieve their goals.

In "20 Lessons from Practical Psychology to Improve Your Life and Achieve Success," we will explore a selection of significant psychological experiments that have shaped our understanding of the human mind. From classic studies to contemporary research, each lesson will reveal valuable insights into how our mind works and how our decisions, beliefs, and emotions can influence our daily lives.

This book not only focuses on the methods and results of these experiments but also emphasizes their practical utility. We will learn how to apply these findings daily, offering concrete strategies to face challenges, improve our relationships, and achieve our aspirations. Through each lesson, you will discover how psychological principles can be implemented in real situations, giving you the tools necessary to promote positive change.

We invite the readers to immerse themselves in the fascinating world of psychology and reflect on their own experiences and behaviors. The lessons presented in this book are designed to inspire, motivate, and guide you on your path to success and self-realization. Join us on this journey of self-discovery and personal growth and become the architect of your own life.

1. Hope is not the last thing to be lost, but the first

Curt Richter's experiment with rats, conducted in the 1950s, is a fascinating example of how hopelessness and hope can dramatically influence survival. The study revealed the powerful psychological impact that the expectation of a rescue or positive outcome has.

The experiment
Curt Richter, a psychobiologist at Johns Hopkins University, conducted a series of experiments with rats submerged in water to measure how long they could swim before giving up and drowning. In the first group, he let the rats swim until they were completely exhausted, and on average, they survived about 15 minutes before giving up and drowning.

However, in a second group of rats, just when it seemed like they were going to give up, Richter took them out of the water, dried them off, and let them rest briefly before returning them to the water. Amazingly, these rats, which had previously seemed on the verge of death, managed to swim not only for another 15 minutes, but some swam for up to 60 hours.

Richter concluded that the rats in the second group, having been rescued once, acquired hope, that is, they hoped that a saving hand would, again, come for them. This temporary rescue gave them the expectation that they could be saved again, and this motivated them to continue swimming much longer than would have been considered possible.

The experiment illustrates that despair is not only about physical condition but that the psyche plays a fundamental role in resilience and the ability to keep fighting in difficult situations. When the rats believed that there was a chance of rescue, their physical endurance increased dramatically.

Lessons for daily life
The power of hope: One of the most important lessons is the impact that hope has on human resilience. In difficult situations, believing that things can get better or that there may be a solution in the future can make the difference between giving up and persevering.

The impact of small victories: Just as the rats that were once rescued managed to swim much longer, in daily life, achieving small achievements or receiving support at key moments can revitalize our energy and give us the strength to continue fighting.

The importance of external support: Just as the rats were rescued at critical moments, in everyday life, people also need support, whether emotional or practical, to cope with moments of crisis. A gesture of help, words of encouragement, or simply being there for someone in a difficult moment can make a significant difference in their ability to move forward.

Resilience is mental and emotional: Resilience is not just physical; mental resilience is essential to persevering through challenges. The belief that current difficulties can change or improve greatly influences a person's ability to endure adverse situations. Cultivating a resilient mindset is key to overcoming obstacles.

The danger of hopelessness: The rats that had no hope gave up in a very short time, showing how devastating hopelessness can be. In human life, feelings of helplessness and a lack of faith in the future can lead to giving up prematurely on situations that could have been solved. It is crucial to recognize these emotional states and work on regaining a positive outlook or asking for help when necessary.

The power of expectation: When we believe that something positive can happen, we are more inclined to try and not give up. This is related to the concept of expectation of success, which suggests that if we believe that our efforts will be rewarded, we are willing to persist longer.

Understanding ideologies: Every ideology (political or religious) has a component of hope, which makes the faithful adhere to it, enduring their current reality, and waiting for a better future.

Practical Application in Daily Life
In the face of problems, seeking hope: Facing difficulties with the belief that there is a solution or that things can improve allows us to find the energy and focus necessary to keep fighting.

Breaking down big goals into small achievements: Like the brief rescue of the rats, achieving small goals can renew our motivation and give us the strength to continue toward larger goals.

Surrounding yourself with supportive people: The people around us influence our ability to overcome challenges. Seeking emotional support and external help in critical moments can be instrumental in keeping us strong.

<u>Developing a resilient mindset:</u> Working on our emotional and mental capacities, such as self-efficacy, hope, and optimism, can prepare us to face adversity more effectively.

Curt Richter's experiment, although simple, is a powerful reminder of how mental state and beliefs about the future can alter our ability to persist, even in extreme situations.

2. Positive Reinforcement Effect

Positive reinforcement is a key concept in the operant conditioning theory developed by psychologist B.F. Skinner. This theory suggests that the consequences of an action influence the likelihood that that action will be repeated in the future. Positive reinforcement occurs when a behavior is followed by a reward or pleasurable stimulus, which increases the likelihood that that behavior will be repeated.

Skinner's Experiment
B.F. Skinner designed a series of experiments using what is known as the "Skinner box" (an operant conditioning chamber) to study how animals learn through the consequences of their actions.

In his best-known experiments, Skinner placed animals, commonly rats or pigeons, inside a box equipped with a lever (for rats) or a disc (for pigeons). Inside the box, the animal could interact with this device and receive a reward, usually food. Skinner observed how the animal's behavior changed based on the consequences of its actions:

Positive reinforcement: If a rat pressed the lever, it received a food pellet. Through repetition of this process, the rat learned that pressing the lever resulted in a reward, so this behavior became more frequent.

Negative reinforcement: In another variation of the experiment, the lever stopped an electric current that was unpleasant for the rat. In this case, the lever-pressing behavior was reinforced because it removed a negative stimulus (the electric current).

<u>Punishment:</u> Skinner also explored how punishment (introduction of a negative stimulus or removal of a positive stimulus) could affect behavior. However, he found that positive reinforcement was more effective at teaching behaviors in the long term.

The experiment showed that when a behavior is followed by a reward (positive reinforcement), the likelihood of that behavior being repeated in the future increases significantly. The rats learned to associate the action of pressing the lever with the consequence of receiving food and therefore did it more frequently.

Lessons for everyday life
Positive reinforcement is a powerful tool not only in animal learning but also in human behavior. The lessons that are derived from this principle have applications in numerous aspects of everyday life:

<u>Encouraging good habits:</u> Positively reinforcing the behaviors we want to see in ourselves, or others is more effective than focusing on punishing the negative. For example, if someone wants to get into the habit of exercising, rewarding themselves with something enjoyable (such as watching an episode of a favorite series) after each exercise session can increase the likelihood of maintaining the habit.

<u>Education and parenting:</u> In early childhood education, rewarding children for positive behaviors, such as sharing, doing homework, or helping around the house, can be much more effective in developing

those behaviors in the long term than punishing them for bad behavior. This also increases the child's self-esteem and fosters a more positive relationship with parents or teachers.

<u>Work Motivation:</u> In the workplace, rewards to reinforce good performance (such as praise, bonuses, or public recognition) can improve employee motivation and increase productivity. Positive reinforcement also creates a more positive work environment, rather than one based on fear of punishment.

<u>Interpersonal Relationships:</u> In personal relationships, reinforcing positive behaviors such as support, empathy, or acts of kindness with expressions of gratitude or affection can strengthen relationships. People tend to repeat behaviors that are well-received or rewarded.

<u>Personal Behavior Management:</u> Positive reinforcement can also be used to modify our behaviors. If we are trying to develop new habits or eliminate unwanted behaviors, rewarding ourselves for small progress can keep us motivated.

<u>Building Self-Esteem:</u> Recognizing and rewarding efforts and accomplishments, rather than focusing on failures, helps build healthy self-esteem. Positive reinforcement not only reinforces behavior but also reinforces belief in one's ability to achieve goals.

The positive reinforcement principle emphasizes that rewarding a desired behavior is a powerful tool for modifying behavior and encouraging learning. Instead of focusing on punishment for undesirable behavior, Skinner showed that rewarding positive behavior leads to better long-term outcomes, both in animal learning and in human behavior. Applying this principle can improve education, personal relationships, work motivation, and the development of good habits in our daily lives.

3. The importance of specific goals

Edwin Locke's Goal Setting Theory, developed in the 1960s, argues that clear, specific goals lead to better performance than vague or indefinite goals. Locke found that setting precise, challenging goals motivates people to try harder, improve their focus, and achieve better results.

Locke's experiment

One of the most representative experiments of this theory was conducted by Locke together with Gary Latham. In this study, Locke observed how workers' performance improved significantly when they were given clear, challenging goals compared to workers who were given easy or vague goals.

Locke and his team experimented with work settings where participants, who were factory workers, were required to complete certain tasks such as assembling parts or producing products on an assembly line. The researchers separated the workers into two groups:

Specific and challenging goal group: This group was given clear, measurable goals, such as producing a specific number of units each time. In addition, these goals were challenging but realistic.

Vague or easy goal group: This group was given more ambiguous instructions, such as "do your best" or "try to increase production," without specifying a concrete objective or measurement standard.

The experiment showed that the group given specific and challenging goals significantly outperformed the group given vague or easy goals. Workers with specific goals achieved higher output worked with greater focus and energy and demonstrated more motivation to improve their performance.

In addition, Locke found that difficult but attainable goals lead to better performance than goals that are too easy. The key was that employees felt they had to work hard to achieve goals, but they knew it was possible to achieve them with enough dedication.

Goal Setting Theory (Key Points)
• Specific goals provide clarity and direction, which helps people focus their efforts.
• Goals should be challenging but achievable, since if a goal is too easy it is not motivating, and if it is too difficult it can be discouraging.
• Feedback is crucial. Locke also stressed that people need to receive feedback on their progress toward the goal to adjust their efforts and stay motivated.
• Goal commitment is important. People must be committed to their goals to achieve higher performance.

Lessons for daily life
Set clear and specific goals: In any aspect of life, whether professional, academic, or personal, vague goals do not lead to action. For example, instead of saying "I want to get fit," a more effective goal would be "I want to run 5 kilometers in under 30 minutes within two months." This goal has a clear objective and a concrete measure.

<u>Challenging goals drive effort:</u> When we set goals that require effort but are attainable, we are more motivated to work hard to achieve them. This applies both at work and in our personal lives. Goals like "learn a new language in 6 months" or "write a book in a year" can be motivating because they are challenging but possible with dedication.

<u>Breaking big goals into sub-goals:</u> A big goal can feel overwhelming. Breaking a goal down into smaller, manageable steps can make progress easier and provide a greater sense of accomplishment. For example, instead of "I want to save up to buy a house," it is more effective to say, "I want to save $500 a month for the next 5 years."

<u>The importance of feedback:</u> To stay motivated, it is essential to track progress toward the goal. If you're working on a long-term project, such as losing weight or developing a new skill, periodically reviewing your progress will allow you to adjust your strategies and stay focused.

<u>Better performance at work and personal life:</u> At work, setting clear, specific goals for yourself or your team can increase productivity. Employees with well-defined goals are often more focused and motivated. In personal life, goals such as improving communication in a relationship or learning to play a musical instrument are best achieved when a clear, measurable action plan is set.

<u>Staying committed to goals:</u> Personal commitment to a goal is key. If a person isn't truly committed to what they've set, they're likely to give up at the first sign of

difficulty. This means that goals should be personally meaningful and align with values and aspirations.

<u>Avoid goals that are too easy</u>: Goals that don't require effort to achieve can reduce motivation. For example, if someone has a natural ability to run, setting a goal of running 1 kilometer won't provide a challenge and won't encourage effort. It's better to set a goal that requires ongoing effort, such as improving time or distance.

Edwin Locke's goal-setting theory teaches that clear, specific, and challenging goals motivate us to perform better and provide a focus for our efforts. In both work and personal life, setting concrete, measurable, and ambitious goals allows us to maximize our performance, while vague goals leave us without direction.

4. Limited self-control

The concept of limited self-control was proposed by psychologist Roy Baumeister based on his research on willpower. Baumeister and his team discovered that self-control functions as a limited resource that can be depleted, a phenomenon he called ego depletion. This study shows that exerting self-control on one task reduces our ability to self-control on subsequent tasks, suggesting that willpower is like a muscle that can become fatigued with constant use.

Baumeister's experiment

One of Baumeister's most well-known experiments was the "Chocolate and Radish Experiment," conducted in the 1990s.

Baumeister gathered a group of college students in a lab and asked them to skip a meal so that they would arrive hungry. He then divided them into two groups:

<u>Radish Group:</u> Participants in this group were presented with a plate of freshly baked chocolate chip cookies and chocolate bonbons, along with a plate of radishes. However, they were asked to only eat the radishes and avoid the sweets. Researchers monitored to ensure that they resisted the temptation to eat the cookies.

<u>Chocolate Group:</u> Participants in this group were allowed to freely eat chocolate chip cookies and bonbons.

After this phase, both groups were required to perform a task that required persistence and concentration, solving a complex puzzle that was impossible to solve. What the researchers wanted to measure was how long the participants persisted before giving up.

The results revealed participants who had exerted self-control by resisting the temptation of cookies (radish group) gave up much sooner on the puzzle task than those who had not had to exert such self-control (chocolate group). On average, those in the radish group persisted for only 8 minutes on the puzzle before giving up, while those in the chocolate group persisted for 19 minutes.

This suggested that self-control had been depleted in the radish group, affecting their ability to continue to face a difficult challenge immediately afterward.

Ego Depletion Theory
Baumeister hypothesized that self-control is a limited resource that, when used, is temporarily depleted, affecting performance on future tasks that also require mental effort or self-control. He called this phenomenon ego depletion.

Lessons for daily life
Baumeister's experiment and the theory of limited self-control have important implications for managing willpower and productivity in daily life. Some key lessons are:

Self-control is a limited resource: Just as muscles get tired after prolonged exertion, our willpower gets depleted with use. If you've been resisting temptations or making difficult decisions all day, you're more likely to give in to temptations later. Being aware of this depletion can help us plan better.

<u>Avoiding excessive decision-making:</u> Decision fatigue is a related phenomenon, where making too many decisions in a short period can deplete our willpower. To avoid this, it's helpful to reduce the number of unnecessary decisions during the day. For example, using a routine for everyday things (like what clothes you wear or what you'll have for breakfast) can free up self-control for more important decisions.

<u>Prioritize the most difficult tasks:</u> If you must do something that requires a lot of self-control, such as working on a complicated task or resisting temptation, do it early in the day when your willpower is at its highest. Easier or less effortful tasks can be left for later when your self-control is at its lowest.

<u>Take breaks to recharge:</u> Self-control can be depleted, but it can also be recharged. Taking short breaks, relaxing, meditating, or simply disconnecting from tasks that require mental effort can restore your ability to control yourself. Just as muscles need rest, so does our willpower.

<u>Recognize the limitations of self-control:</u> Being aware that your willpower can be depleted allows you to be more compassionate with yourself. If you are in a moment of weakness, it doesn't mean you lack self-control altogether, but perhaps you have temporarily depleted it. Instead of blaming yourself, look for ways to restore it, such as resting or planning your time better.

Develop self-control like a muscle: Although self-control can be depleted, it can also be strengthened with practice. If you consistently expose yourself to situations that require small doses of self-control and gradually increase the challenge, you can increase your ability to handle difficult situations over the long term.

Eat and rest well: Baumeister's research also suggests that glucose is an important fuel for self-control. Maintaining stable energy levels through good eating and rest is essential to sustaining self-control. Avoiding long workdays without eating or sleep deprivation reduces the ability to make good decisions and resist temptations.

Simplicity in routines: Baumeister notes that successful people often eliminate the need to make many decisions by structuring their lives in simple ways. For example, characters like Steve Jobs or Mark Zuckerberg adopted repetitive wardrobes to minimize trivial decision-making, reserving their energy for important decisions.

Baumeister's study of limited self-control demonstrates that willpower is a finite resource that can be temporarily depleted but can also be managed and strengthened. In daily life, it is crucial to learn to manage our self-control, recognize when we are mentally exhausted, and structure our tasks in a way that we avoid fatigue. Strategies to recharge our willpower and reduce unnecessary decision-making can help us be more effective and successful in our goals.

5. Social pressure influences decisions

Solomon Asch's conformity experiment, conducted in the 1950s, is one of the most famous studies of how social pressure can influence people's decisions, even when these decisions go against what they know to be right. Asch showed that under certain conditions, individuals can conform to the opinion of the group, even if this opinion is incorrect.

The Asch experiment

Asch's goal was to investigate the extent to which people would give in to group pressure when making decisions, even when the correct answer was obvious.

The experiment involved a group of 7-9 people, but only one of them was the actual subject of the study; the rest were confederates of the experimenter (known as confederates). The participants sat in a room and were shown a series of cards with lines of different lengths. The task was simple: determine which of three lines (A, B, or C) was the same length as a reference line.

The confederates, following instructions from the researcher, responded incorrectly in several rounds of the experiment. That is, they deliberately chose an incorrect line, but unanimously.

The real subject responded at the end of the line, after hearing the incorrect answers from the others. The key question was whether the person would dare to give the correct answer, in contradiction to the group, or whether he or she would conform to the group's wrong answer.

On control trials (when confederates gave no incorrect answers), subjects almost always responded correctly. However, when confederates gave incorrect answers, approximately 75% of participants conformed with the majority at least once, giving the incorrect answer that the group had given. On average, subjects conformed in 37% of the critical trials.

Most tellingly, many of the participants knew that the group's answer was wrong, but still decided to conform. Some of those who confirmed reported that they did so to avoid being the "only one" who disagreed or to not appear "different," while others began to doubt their perception under group pressure.

Asch concluded that peer pressure has a powerful effect on individual decisions, even when people know the group is wrong. Conformity occurs for several reasons:

<u>Desire for acceptance:</u> People don't want to be seen as different or disruptive, so they conform to the majority to avoid rejection.

<u>Self-doubt:</u> Sometimes peer pressure is so strong that people begin to question their perception and come to believe the group must be right.

<u>Conflict avoidance:</u> In many cases, conformity is a strategy to avoid conflict or confrontation, as disagreeing with a group can lead to social tension.

Lessons for everyday life

The influence of the group is powerful: This experiment highlights the impact peer pressure can have on everyday decisions. In situations such as group elections, team decisions, or even personal issues, majority opinions can exert great pressure, even if they are not correct. This is relevant in both social and professional settings.

Questioning group opinion: It is important to maintain a critical perspective when faced with group opinion. Although the desire to belong to a group is natural, we should not sacrifice our judgments and convictions if we know something is wrong. Developing the ability to resist conformity is essential to maintaining personal integrity and making more authentic choices.

The importance of self-confidence: The Asch experiment shows how self-doubt can arise under social pressure. In situations where there is pressure to follow the majority, it is crucial to trust one's perception and judgment, especially when there is clear evidence of what is right. Building confidence in our abilities can help us resist the urge to blindly conform.

Conformity can be destructive: In some situations, blindly following the majority can lead to bad decisions, both on a personal and societal level. This can include financial, ethical, or moral decisions. For example, conformity at work could lead to accepting unethical practices because "everyone else is doing it." Being able to maintain an ethical stance despite peer pressure is crucial to responsible decision-making.

Avoiding unreflective group decision-making: The phenomenon of group conformity can be especially damaging in situations where deliberation and critical thinking are necessary, such as in trials, political decisions, or business. This is known as the groupthink phenomenon, where people within a group tend to suppress their individual opinions so as not to disturb the harmony of the group. Making group decisions requires that each member feels empowered to express his or her opinion honestly, even if it differs from the rest.

Strengthening critical thinking in young people: In the field of education and parenting, it is important to teach young people to be critical in the face of social pressure. This experiment has implications for how we educate the new generations so that they do not just accept the default norm, but also question what the group says or does if it goes against their values.

Becoming aware of social bias: Being aware of how social pressure can influence our perception is a first step in resisting it. Recognizing the tendency to conform under certain circumstances allows us to be alerted to avoid blindly following the flow, and thus be able to make more conscious decisions.

Creating spaces for dissent: In personal or professional relationships, it is essential to create an environment where people feel comfortable expressing their disagreement. Fostering a space where people are not penalized for having a different opinion can lead to more balanced and well-thought-out decisions.

The Asch conformity experiment shows how powerful social pressure can be in influencing our decisions, even when we know we are right. Conformity can arise from a desire for acceptance, doubt about our perceptions, or a desire to avoid conflict. The lessons that are derived from this experiment highlight the importance of maintaining a critical stance, developing self-confidence, and resisting the pressure to blindly follow the majority. In everyday life, we must cultivate independent thinking and create spaces where divergent opinions are valued.

6. The Pygmalion Effect

The Pygmalion Effect is a psychological phenomenon that demonstrates how one person's expectations of another can influence the latter's behavior, leading them to meet those expectations, whether positive or negative. This concept was investigated by psychologists Robert Rosenthal and Lenore Jacobson in an experiment they conducted in the 1960s, focusing on the impact of teachers' expectations on students' academic performance.

The Rosenthal and Jacobson Experiment

The study was conducted in an elementary school and its goal was to observe how teachers' expectations influenced students' performance.

Intelligence Test: At the beginning of the school year, Rosenthal and Jacobson administered an intelligence test to all students in the school. However, they did not reveal the actual results to the teachers. Instead, they randomly selected a group of students and told the teachers that these children were "outstanding students" or that they showed extraordinary potential to make remarkable academic development during the year.

Teachers' expectations: The teachers did not know that the students were randomly selected, so they assumed that the children who were singled out had high potential. This change in the teachers' perceptions led to different expectations for those students, even though there was no difference in their initial abilities.

<u>Final assessment:</u> At the end of the school year, the students were given the intelligence test again, and the results showed that the children who had been labeled "promising" by the teachers significantly improved their academic performance compared to the others.

The study showed that the students who were labeled "promising" at random (without any basis in their previous performance) improved markedly in their academic performance. This was not due to any real difference in the children's abilities, but rather to the higher expectations that the teachers had for them. Teachers unconsciously provided more attention, support, and encouragement to those students, which in turn increased the children's motivation and performance.

The study revealed that the expectations of others can deeply influence a person's behavior and performance. In this case, teachers' positive expectations of students led to children performing better academically. This is called the Pygmalion Effect, about the Greek myth of Pygmalion, a sculptor who fell in love with a statue he had created, which came to life because he believed in its perfection.

This effect applies not only to academic contexts, but to many areas of life, including work, personal relationships, and individual development. The positive or negative expectations that others have of us can influence how we act and the results we achieve.

Lessons for daily life
<u>Expectations have power:</u> The expectations we have about others can directly influence how they behave. If

we expect a person to fail or struggle, these expectations are likely to become reality. On the other hand, if we expect someone to succeed, we are more likely to see that success manifest itself.

<u>The impact of expectations on education</u>: Teachers and educators need to be aware of the impact their expectations have on student performance. Treating all students as capable and promising can increase their motivation and performance while having low expectations can limit their potential.

<u>How expectations shape personal relationships</u>: In our relationships, the expectations we have about our friends, family, or partners can influence the dynamics of the relationship. For example, if we believe that someone will always disappoint us, we are likely to begin behaving in ways that increase the likelihood of that happening. In contrast, if we believe in the growth and potential of others, we can positively influence their behavior and help them achieve their goals.

<u>Self-Expectations</u>: The Pygmalion Effect can also apply to oneself. The expectations we have about our performance influence how we behave. If we believe we are not capable of achieving something, we are likely not to put in the effort necessary to achieve it. Conversely, if we are confident in our abilities and that we can improve, that confidence will lead to better results.

<u>Motivation in the Workplace</u>: In the workplace, expectations from supervisors and coworkers can influence employee performance. Leaders who show confidence in their teams' abilities and offer positive

feedback can inspire better results, while those who constantly underestimate or criticize their employees can create an environment of low performance.

Reverse Pygmalion Effect: It is important to recognize that this phenomenon can also work in a negative way, which is known as the Golem Effect. This occurs when the low expectations of a person (such as a teacher or boss) decrease someone's performance or motivation. If we believe someone is incapable, that belief can lead them to behave in a way that meets those negative expectations.

The Importance of Positive Reinforcement: If we want to motivate others to improve, it is essential to focus on their strengths and potential, rather than highlighting their weaknesses. Positive reinforcement, when sincere and constructive, can create an environment in which people feel valued and willing to try harder.

Model high but realistic expectations: Although the Pygmalion Effect can be powerful, it is essential to set high but realistic expectations. If expectations are too high or unrealistic, they can have the opposite effect and lead to frustration. The balance between motivation and reality is key to achieving positive results.

Set positive expectations in children: Parents can apply this effect in raising their children. Setting positive (but achievable) expectations for children in terms of behavior, academic performance, or personal development can foster their confidence and willingness to learn and grow.

<u>Language matters:</u> The words and language we use to describe others also influence their behaviors. Telling someone capable and talented can shape their self-concept, while repeated negative feedback can erode a person's confidence.

The Pygmalion Effect, as demonstrated by Rosenthal and Jacobson, reveals the power of expectations in shaping people's performance and behavior. Whether in education, work, or personal relationships, our beliefs and perceptions about others can influence their success or failure. By cultivating positive and realistic expectations for others and us, we can help unlock potential and bring about positive changes in our lives and the lives of those around us.

7. Systematic Desensitization to Overcome Fears

Systematic desensitization is a therapeutic technique used to help people overcome phobias and fears by gradually exposing them to anxiety-provoking stimuli. One of the first experiments using a similar technique was conducted by Mary Cover Jones in the 1920s. She is often considered the "mother of behavioral therapy," and her work pioneered the treatment of childhood phobias.

Mary Cover Jones' Experiment

Mary Cover Jones was a psychologist who worked on an experiment with a boy named Peter, who had an intense fear of rabbits. Her goal was to eliminate the boy's fear through a process of controlled exposure, laying the groundwork for what would later be known as systematic desensitization.

<u>Fear Assessment</u>: Peter, a young boy, had an extreme fear of rabbits. Jones observed that when Peter saw a rabbit, he began to show signs of fear and avoidance.

<u>Gradual exposure:</u> To help Peter overcome his fear, Jones designed a plan in which the rabbit would be progressively brought closer while Peter was in a comfortable and relaxing environment. Peter was also given his favorite food, which created a positive experience that countered his anxiety.

At first, the rabbit was far away from Peter, outside his immediate fear zone, and while Peter was eating, the animal remained in a visible but distant area.

Gradually, over time and repeated encounters, the rabbit would slowly come closer to Peter, without the boy panicking. Each time Peter became more comfortable, the rabbit would come a little closer.

<u>Positive association:</u> During the process, Peter was not only exposed to the rabbit but was also given pleasant experiences (his favorite food) so that he would associate the rabbit's presence with something positive rather than fear.

<u>Outcome</u>: After several sessions, Peter became comfortable enough to touch and interact with the rabbit, indicating that his fear had been significantly reduced. Through this process of gradual and repetitive exposure, Peter was desensitized to the rabbit.

Mary Cover Jones' experiment showed that gradual exposure to a feared object, along with positive association, could help reduce or eliminate fear. This innovative approach laid the groundwork for behavioral therapy and systematic desensitization, a method that has been widely used to treat phobias today.

Systematic desensitization is based on the idea that anxiety and fear can be eliminated if people gradually face their fears, but in a way that allows them to maintain control and reduce anxiety. The goal is for the person to associate exposure to the feared object or situation with a relaxed response, rather than one of panic or fear.

Typical steps of systematic desensitization

Relaxation: The first step is to teach the person relaxation techniques, such as deep breathing or progressive muscle relaxation. This is crucial, as it helps reduce overall anxiety during the exposure process.

Fear hierarchy: The person and therapist create a list of situations that generate fear, ordered from least to most intense. For example, if someone is afraid of flying, the first step might be talking about airplanes, then looking at pictures, and then getting on a plane.

Gradual exposure: The person is gradually exposed to the objects or situations on the list, starting with those that generate the least fear. While being exposed to each situation, the person uses relaxation techniques to stay calm.

Progress: As the person becomes more comfortable with lower levels of anxiety, they move on to situations that generate more fear, until they are finally able to face the greatest fear without experiencing significant anxiety.

Lessons for daily life

Facing fears step by step: One of the most important lessons from Mary Cover Jones' experiment is that fears can be overcome progressively. Instead of avoiding what we fear, it is more effective to face fears gradually. Breaking a big challenge down into smaller steps makes it more manageable and less overwhelming.

<u>Positive association can transform fear</u>: The technique Jones used with Peter, combining exposure to the feared object with positive stimuli, shows that you can reframe the perception of a frightening experience by associating pleasant feelings with it. In everyday life, this suggests that you can change the way you view something frightening by incorporating pleasant or relaxing experiences into that situation.

<u>The power of relaxation</u>: Systematic desensitization underscores the importance of learning to relax in times of anxiety. Techniques such as deep breathing or muscle relaxation can be useful tools for managing anxiety and stress. Facing fears with a calmer mindset helps reduce the intensity of emotional reactions.

<u>Overcoming avoidance:</u> Many people tend to avoid situations that cause fear, which can make the problem worse in the long run. The key lesson here is that avoidance perpetuates fear while facing it (even gradually) allows you to overcome it. This is applicable in many aspects of life, from specific phobias to more general fears, such as fear of failure or public speaking.

<u>The importance of persistence:</u> The experiment shows that change does not happen overnight, but that with patience and persistence, fears can fade away. This principle is applicable in many areas of life: problems may seem insurmountable at first, but with time and consistent focus, they can be overcome.

<u>Reframing failure:</u> Many times, fear is linked to the possibility of failure. Learning to see failure not as something catastrophic but as a part of the learning process allows us to move forward without being

paralyzed by fear. Gradual desensitization teaches us that each step, no matter how small, brings us closer to overcoming our fears.

<u>Social support and safe environment:</u> In the experiment, Peter was in a safe environment and surrounded by support as he faced his fear of the rabbit. This highlights the importance of having a supportive environment when trying to overcome a personal challenge. Having friends, family, or mentors who encourage and reassure us can make a huge difference in our growth process.

<u>Managing anxiety on a day-to-day basis:</u> Desensitization techniques not only apply to specific fears but can also help people deal with everyday anxiety. By gradually confronting situations that cause stress, such as public speaking, job interviews, or difficult social interactions, greater resilience and confidence can be developed.

Mary Cover Jones' experiment with the boy Peter was a crucial step in the development of behavioral therapy and systematic desensitization. Through gradual exposure and positive association, it is possible to overcome deep-rooted fears and phobias. In daily life, this technique teaches the importance of progressively facing fears, staying calm in stressful situations, and cultivating persistence in the process of self-improvement.

8. The Power of Environment on Behavior

The Stanford Prison Experiment, conducted in 1971 by psychologist Philip Zimbardo, is one of the most famous studies on how environment and social roles can profoundly influence human behavior. Through this experiment, Zimbardo demonstrated that even "normal" people can behave in an abusive or submissive manner depending on the circumstances and environment they find themselves in.

Description of the experiment

The goal of the experiment was to understand the psychological effects of incarceration on both prisoners and guards. Zimbardo wanted to see to what extent assigned social roles and the environment of a prison influenced the behavior of ordinary people.

Selection of participants: 24 mentally and physically healthy male volunteers were selected through a newspaper advertisement. Participants were randomly assigned to play the roles of guards or prisoners in a simulated prison in the basement of the psychology building at Stanford University. All participants knew it was an experiment and were paid to participate.

Setting up the environment: A mock prison was built in the basement of the university, with cells for the prisoners and control areas for the guards. The prisoners were given uniforms, and identification numbers, and were arrested at home by local police as part of the immersion process. The guards were also given uniforms, reflective sunglasses (to prevent eye contact), and batons, giving them an appearance of authority.

Start of the experiment: The experiment was planned to last two weeks. However, it began to take an unexpected turn almost immediately. The guards, who had complete authority over the prisoners, began to abuse their power, imposing psychological and physical punishments. For their part, the prisoners began to show signs of depression, anxiety, and submission, and some even began to have emotional breakdowns.

Behavioral evolution:

The guards: Although the guards knew they were participating in an experiment, many of them began to act sadistically, humiliating and mistreating the prisoners. They implemented arbitrary rules, such as forcing prisoners to do excessive physical exercises, restricting their use of the bathroom, or keeping them awake for long periods.

The prisoners: The prisoners, for their part, began to feel truly trapped, even though they knew they could leave the experiment at any time. They began to accept the guards' abuse, showing submission and resignation, with some prisoners even developing passive and depressive behaviors.

Discontinuation of the experiment: The experiment, which was scheduled to last 14 days, had to be interrupted on the sixth day due to the extent of the psychological deterioration of both the prisoners and the guards. One of Zimbardo's colleagues, along with his girlfriend, visited the simulated prison and convinced him that the experiment had gone too far and should be stopped.

The Stanford Prison Experiment showed the extent to which social roles and environment can influence human behavior. Even people considered "normal" and psychologically stable can act cruelly or submissively when they are assigned certain roles and placed in an environment of authority and subordination. Zimbardo concluded that human behavior is highly influenced by the social context and expectations associated with the roles people adopt.

Lessons for daily life

<u>The power of the environment:</u> This experiment demonstrates that the environment has a huge impact on people's behavior. Even if we are aware of what is right or wrong, our behavior can change drastically in an environment that promotes or allows abusive behavior. This underscores the importance of healthy environments, whether at work, school or in personal relationships. To avoid destructive behavior, it is vital to create environments that promote respect and ethics.

<u>Dehumanization:</u> The experiment showed how guards began to dehumanize prisoners, seeing them more as "objects" than as human beings. This is a phenomenon that can occur in real life, especially in situations of unbalanced power, such as in military institutions, businesses, prisons, or abusive situations. It is important to remember that regardless of role or position, we are all human beings, and dehumanization can lead to harmful and abusive behavior.

<u>The danger of unchecked authority:</u> The experiment highlights the danger of giving people too much power

without oversight or control. In everyday life, this can be seen in many hierarchical systems, such as the work environment, where bosses or leaders can abuse their power if there are no oversight mechanisms in place. Accountability and oversight are essential to prevent power from being used in destructive ways.

<u>The influence of social roles</u>: Social roles have a strong influence on how we act. Sometimes, the expectations associated with a role can lead us to behave in ways we would never have imagined outside of that role. For example, a person who takes on the role of "boss" may start to act more authoritarian or even abusive, even though they are kind in their personal life. It is essential to be aware of how roles can influence our actions and to make sure that we do not justify inappropriate behavior simply because we are in a position of power.

<u>Conformity and social pressure:</u> The behavior of prisoners showed how people can accept abusive or humiliating situations under social pressure or when they feel they have no control. This conformity to authority may explain why, in everyday life, people sometimes do not report abuse or injustice. It is important to recognize when we are being negatively conformist and find the courage to stand up to wrong situations.

<u>The ability to act against our values:</u> The experiment showed that, under the right circumstances, people who would normally behave ethically can act against their values. This is applicable in everyday life in pressure situations, where we can be influenced to act in ways that do not reflect our principles. Being aware

of this fact can help us resist the pressure to act in ways we know are wrong.

<u>The importance of reflection and external intervention</u>: Zimbardo, who was acting as the prison warden, became so involved in the experiment that he did not realize the psychological damage that was taking place until an outside observer pointed it out to him. This teaches that, in everyday life, critical reflection and external input are essential to avoid falling into harmful dynamics. Having people outside the system who can objectively observe and evaluate a situation can prevent abuses.

<u>The fragile nature of morality</u>: The study reveals how fragile human morality can be under certain conditions. We often believe that our principles are firm, but this experiment suggests that our decisions can be strongly influenced by our environment and circumstances. Therefore, it is essential to maintain self-awareness and constantly question our actions and the environment we are in.

<u>Personal responsibility:</u> Zimbardo's experiment illustrates the human tendency to justify inappropriate behaviors on the grounds of "following orders" or fulfilling a role. However, a key lesson is that each person is responsible for their actions, regardless of the context they are in. In daily life, we must be aware of our ability to influence others and our moral responsibilities.

<u>Systems and structures matter as much as people:</u> This experiment also highlights that it is not just individual people who determine behavior, but the

systems and structures in which they operate. A poorly designed system, such as an abusive prison or a toxic work environment, can encourage negative behaviors. Therefore, to improve human behavior, we must not only focus on people but also on improving the systems in which they operate.

The Stanford Prison Experiment is a dramatic example of how the environment and social roles can shape human behavior in ways that are not always positive. This study teaches us to be aware of how power, social context, and authority can influence our actions and underscores the importance of self-awareness, monitoring, and creating ethical and fair environments.

9. The Importance of Self-Perception

Self-perception theory, proposed by social psychologist Daryl Bem in the 1970s, suggests that people infer their attitudes, emotions, and motivations by observing their behavior, like how they observe others to understand them. Rather than relying on deep introspections, self-perception is based on the analysis of our actions and the circumstances in which they occur. This theory is particularly useful in explaining how we form attitudes about ambiguous or unclear issues, and how we come to know ourselves through observing what we do.

Daryl Bem's Experiment

Bem developed a series of studies to demonstrate how people develop attitudes based on observing their behavior. One of the key experiments was like Leon Festinger's classic experiment on cognitive dissonance but with a different interpretation.

<u>Participants:</u> Participants in the study performed a boring, repetitive task, like the one in Festinger's study (where subjects turned knobs for an hour). After completing the task, some participants received a small monetary reward, while others received a larger reward for lying to a fictitious participant and telling them that the task was fun.

Experimental conditions:

One group received $1 to lie about the task, which represented a low reward.

Another group received $20, which represented a much higher reward.

<u>Behavioral observation</u>: Bem argued that subjects who received a small amount of money (just $1) came to convince themselves that they enjoyed the task because they did not have sufficient external justification (i.e., the low payoff) to lie. In contrast, the group that received $20 had a clear external justification for lying, so they did not need to change their internal perception of the boring task.

<u>Self-perception:</u> According to Bem, participants who received only $1 observed their behavior (lying for a small amount of money) and, to justify their action, concluded that they must have enjoyed the task. This is an example of self-perception: people observe their actions and circumstances and deduce what their true feelings or attitudes must be.

The experiment showed that people, instead of looking introspect to find out what they feel, can simply observe what they do and then deduce what their attitudes must be. In this case, those who received only $1 deducted that, if they lied for so little money, they probably must have enjoyed the task.

Self-perception vs. Cognitive Dissonance Theory

Although Festinger's Cognitive Dissonance Theory argues that people change their attitudes to reduce internal discomfort between their actions and their beliefs, Bem proposed an alternative: people do not need to experience dissonance, but simply observe their behavior to deduce what their attitudes are. According to Bem, people may not have direct access to their internal emotions or attitudes, and instead of introspecting, they simply analyze their actions.

Lessons for Daily Life

<u>Behavior influences our beliefs:</u> Self-perception theory teaches us that our actions can influence our attitudes and beliefs more than we imagine. For example, if we start acting positively toward something (such as exercising regularly), we are likely to, over time, begin to believe that we enjoy that activity. In daily life, this suggests that behaving proactively or positively can change our internal attitudes, even if we don't initially feel that way.

<u>Fake it till you feel it:</u> A key lesson is the phrase "fake it till you feel it." If we engage in behaviors that are aligned with how we want to feel (for example, being nice to others or being confident in social situations), our internal emotions can align with those behaviors. Instead of waiting to feel a certain way before acting, we can act first and let our attitudes follow our actions.

<u>External rewards can interfere with internal enjoyment:</u> Bem's experiment also teaches us that when our actions are primarily motivated by external rewards (such as money, praise, or recognition), we are less likely to develop internal motivation. Instead, when external rewards are minimal, we tend to justify our actions internally, which can increase our sense of enjoyment or commitment toward the activity. In daily life, this means that we should avoid relying too heavily on external rewards if we want to cultivate stronger internal motivations.

Get to know yourself through your actions: Self-perception theory suggests that we can learn more about ourselves by observing our behavior. If we are unsure of how we feel about something (such as a relationship or a job), we can observe how we act in those situations and draw conclusions from our behavior. This can be helpful when we lack emotional clarity, as our actions can reveal to us what we think or feel.

How to handle changing attitudes: If we want to change a negative attitude, a good strategy may be to start with small behavioral changes that reflect the attitude we want to have. For example, if we want to be more open to new experiences, we might start by trying activities we would normally avoid. According to self-perception theory, our mind will deduce from our actions that we should be more open than we thought.

External justifications can backfire: If we offer people excessive external justifications (such as large rewards or punishments) for doing something, they are less likely to develop a positive internal attitude toward that activity. This applies in parenting, education, and work: Instead of over-rewarding children or employees for their actions, it is better to foster internal motivation for them to develop positive attitudes on their own.

The importance of consistency between behavior and attitudes: Often, our actions influence how we perceive ourselves. If we are consistent in performing certain behaviors, we are likely to begin to believe that those actions reflect who we are. This underscores the importance of aligning our behavior with the attitudes we want to cultivate in ourselves.

The plasticity of our beliefs: Self-perception theory also shows that our beliefs are not fixed; they can change based on how we act. While we sometimes think we must have a certain attitude or belief to act a certain way, the reality is that we can modify our attitudes by changing our behavior. In daily life, this helps overcome limiting beliefs or negative attitudes toward us or others.

The impact of small actions: We do not need to make big changes to influence our beliefs and attitudes. The small actions we take in our day-to-day lives, such as smiling more or being more generous, can have a cumulative effect on our perception of ourselves. This highlights the importance of paying attention to small behaviors and how they influence our self-perception.

How to improve self-confidence: If we feel insecure or lack confidence in certain areas, an effective way to increase confidence is to start acting confidently, even if we don't feel that way at first. Self-perception theory suggests that by behaving confidently, we will eventually come to see ourselves as more confident people than we initially believed.

Daryl Bem's Self-Perception Theory offers valuable insight into how our actions influence our beliefs and attitudes. Rather than relying solely on introspection to understand ourselves, we can often learn more by observing our behavior. This theory teaches us that our attitudes and beliefs are not static but can change based on our actions. In everyday life, this theory suggests that if we want to change our attitude toward something, it is helpful to start by changing our behavior, and that acting as if we already have the desired attitude can lead us to develop that attitude internally.

10. The Placebo Effect

The placebo effect is a psychological and physiological phenomenon in which a person experiences an improvement in their health or well-being after receiving an inactive or fake treatment (the "placebo"), simply because they believe they are receiving an effective intervention. This effect has been the subject of numerous studies in psychology and medicine, as it illustrates the power of the mind to influence the perception of pain, illness, and healing.

Experiments on the Placebo Effect
One of the most famous experiments studying the placebo effect was conducted in the field of medicine. In many clinical studies, researchers compare a real treatment to a placebo to determine the effectiveness of the treatment in question. A typical experiment involving the placebo effect is described below.

Participants: A group of patients suffering from a medical condition, such as chronic pain, insomnia, or depression, was selected for the study. These patients did not know whether they would receive the real treatment or a placebo.

Experimental conditions:

One group of participants received a real drug to treat their condition (such as a painkiller, antidepressant, etc.).

Another group received a placebo pill, which contained no active ingredient but which they were told was an effective treatment.

Procedure: None of the participants knew whether they were receiving the real drug or the placebo (a double-blind design). In addition, participants were informed about the possible positive effects of the "drug" they would receive, which created expectations of improvement in both groups.

Results: Surprisingly, in many studies of this type, a significant proportion of people who received the placebo reported improvements in their condition, often to almost the same degree as those who took the real drug. Participants reported less pain, improved mood, and reduced other symptoms, even though the placebo contained no active ingredient.

The placebo effect is not just psychological; it can trigger real physiological responses in the body. Researchers have found that when people believe they are receiving effective treatment, their brains release chemicals such as endorphins and dopamine, which can relieve pain and improve well-being. In addition, the immune system and other bodily systems may react positively due to the expectation of healing.

One of the most significant studies on the placebo effect was by Henry Beecher, a doctor during World War II who observed that wounded soldiers experienced pain relief even when he gave them a saline solution instead of morphine, due to the belief that they were receiving a powerful painkiller. This finding led to increased interest in researching the role of placebo in medicine.

Lessons for daily life

<u>The power of expectations:</u> The placebo effect teaches us that our expectations have a profound impact on how we feel. If we believe that something will help us or make us feel better, our brain can activate healing mechanisms that improve our well-being. In daily life, this reminds us that our mental attitudes and expectations can influence our success, happiness, and health. A positive mindset and belief in success or recovery can help us achieve better outcomes in many aspects of life.

<u>The mind-body connection:</u> The placebo effect demonstrates the deep connection between the mind and the body. Positive beliefs can trigger physiological responses that lead to real improvement. This helps remember that emotional state can have an impact on physical health. Maintaining an optimistic attitude or using strategies such as meditation or relaxation to reduce stress can have beneficial effects on health.

<u>Self-care can be powerful:</u> The simple act of taking care of yourself (for example, taking a supplement, exercising, or following a healthy routine) can reap benefits because it creates the expectation of well-being. Even if the treatment itself is not miraculous, the act of focusing on your health and well-being can bring about positive changes, both psychologically and physically. This underscores the importance of believing in the efforts we make for our well-being.

<u>Confidence in treatments:</u> One of the important lessons of the placebo effect is that patients who trust their treatment tend to show better results. This is also applicable to other areas of life: if we trust the processes we follow to improve in any area (work, relationships, skills), we are more likely to obtain positive results. Belief in the process or path we are taking can enhance the real benefits.

<u>Beware of excessive medication or treatments:</u> The placebo effect also teaches us that many times, expensive or aggressive treatments are not necessary if people have a positive expectation of improvement. This can be applied in daily life by remembering that many times we do not need drastic or expensive solutions to solve a problem; a positive mindset and simple solutions can be enough.

<u>The value of words and environment:</u> Part of the success of the placebo effect is due to how doctors present the treatments. The words of encouragement, security, and confidence are transmitted by a professional influence on the patient's expectation of improvement. This can be applied to daily life in the way we speak to others and how we create a positive environment. Words of encouragement and optimistic expectations can have a significant impact on the confidence and performance of those around us.

<u>Self-efficacy and personal beliefs:</u> The placebo effect also reinforces the idea of self-efficacy or the belief in our ability to handle situations and overcome challenges. If we believe we can improve, whether in our health or other areas of life, we are more inclined to take actions that reinforce that belief. This teaches

us that cultivating a growth mindset and confidence in our abilities is key to success and well-being.

The importance of social support: Studies on the placebo effect also show that supportive environments and empathy influence the effectiveness of the placebo. In daily life, this highlights the importance of surrounding ourselves with people who support us emotionally and who reinforce our positive beliefs. Environment and social support have a direct impact on how we feel and our ability to overcome difficulties.

The placebo effect offers us a powerful lesson about the mind's role in healing and well-being. Through positive expectations, the mind-body connection, and a supportive environment, people can experience real improvements in their health without the need for active treatment. The lessons of the placebo effect are applicable not only in medicine, but in everyday life, highlighting the importance of our beliefs, attitudes, and the environment in which we develop. In short, the mind has a remarkable power to influence our reality, and learning to harness that power can improve both our health and our overall well-being.

11. Priming Effect

The priming effect is a psychological phenomenon that refers to how exposure to one stimulus (word, image, sound, etc.) can influence a person's response to a subsequent stimulus, without this influence being conscious. This concept is based on the idea that our minds are interconnected, and that recent information can affect our thinking and behavior in subtle ways.

The Priming Experiment by Bargh et al. (1996)

One of the best-known experiments demonstrating the priming effect was conducted by John Bargh and his colleagues in 1996. In this study, they investigated how exposure to words related to aging could influence participants' behavior.

Participants: Researchers recruited college students to participate in an experiment on "language and personality."

Priming: Participants were given a series of words to form sentences. There were two groups:

Group 1 (Old-Age Priming): Received words related to old age (e.g., "wise," "granny," "gray-haired," "recline").

Group 2 (Control Group): Received neutral words that were not related to old age (e.g., "table," "bird," "spoon," "sky").

Behavioral Measurement: After completing the sentence formation task, participants were asked to walk from the lab to the elevator. The time it took them to get to the elevator was measured. The researchers expected that participants who had been exposed to the old-age priming would move more slowly, compared to those who had not received the priming.

Results: The results showed that participants who had been exposed to old-age-related words did indeed walk more slowly to the elevator compared to those who did not receive the priming. This showed that simply thinking about old age affected their behavior unconsciously.

Lessons for daily life
Influence of stimuli on our behavior: The priming effect teaches us that our actions and decisions can be influenced by stimuli that we are not aware of having received. Therefore, it is important to be aware of our environment and the messages we are exposed to, as they can impact our perceptions and behaviors without us knowing it.

Creating a positive environment: Since priming can influence our emotions and behaviors, creating a positive and motivating environment can help us have a better mood and be more productive. For example, surrounding yourself with images, words, or music that evoke feelings of happiness and success can improve your mindset and performance.

The importance of language: The words we use and are exposed to can have a significant impact on our behavior and mindset. Using positive and motivating language, both in our internal communication and in our interactions with others, can foster a healthier and more positive mindset. This is applicable in work, educational, and personal settings.

Effects on decision-making: Priming can affect our purchasing decisions and the choices we make. For example, advertisements often use priming to influence our preferences, either through positive images or keywords. Being aware of this technique allows us to make more informed decisions that are less influenced by external stimuli.

Influencing social behavior: In social situations, expectations and the context in which we interact with others can influence how we perceive and treat people. For example, if we are in an environment that values kindness and respect, we are likely to behave kinder. Fostering a positive social environment can improve our interactions and relationships with others.

Study and learning techniques: The priming effect can also be applied in the educational setting. For example, educators can use priming techniques to help students remember information related to a topic by presenting keywords or concepts before the lesson. This can facilitate learning and retention of information.

Self-care and mindset: We can use priming in our everyday lives to encourage healthy habits and a positive mindset. For example, by practicing positive affirmations or visualizing successful outcomes, we can influence our mindset and motivation to achieve our goals.

Being proactive about external influence: Being aware of the priming effect allows us to be proactive in how we expose ourselves to stimuli. This includes carefully choosing the media we consume, the music we listen to, and the conversations we engage in. By selecting positive and uplifting information, we can improve our overall well-being.

The priming effect reveals how our thoughts and behaviors can be influenced by external stimuli in subtle and unconscious ways. This phenomenon has important implications in our daily lives, from how we behave and make decisions to how we can create an environment that fosters well-being and personal growth. By being aware of priming and its effects, we can design our environment and interactions in ways that support a positive and productive mindset.

12. The anchoring effect

The anchoring effect is a cognitive bias identified by psychologists Daniel Kahneman and Amos Tversky in which people over-rely on the first piece of information they receive (the "anchor") when making decisions. This first number or piece of information influences their subsequent decisions, although the additional information they receive should lead them to reconsider their judgment. Anchoring is an automatic process that occurs in our minds and affects our ability to reason and judge.

The Kahneman and Tversky Experiment

Kahneman and Tversky conducted a series of experiments that demonstrated how anchoring can influence decisions, even when people know that the initial anchor is irrelevant.

Participants: Participants were asked to estimate numerical answers to general knowledge questions. For example, in one of the experiments they were asked what the percentage of African countries in the United Nations was.

The anchor process:

Before responding, participants saw a randomly generated number by spinning a wheel (which was rigged to stop at either the number 10 or 65).

After seeing the number, they were asked to respond whether they thought the percentage of African countries in the UN was higher or lower than the number presented by the wheel.

They were then asked to give a numerical estimate of the actual percentage.

Results: Even though the number on the wheel was completely irrelevant to the question, participants who had seen the number 10 gave significantly lower estimates than those who had seen the number 65. This showed that the initial (anchor) number influenced subsequent responses, even when they knew the number had no bearing on the question.

Lessons for everyday life

The first piece of information matters more than we think: The anchoring effect teaches us that the first number or piece of information we receive tends to have a disproportionate impact on our decisions. This applies in areas such as salary negotiations, where the initial offer can anchor the rest of the discussion, or in pricing in sales, where the first price seen establishes a mental reference. In everyday life, it is important to be aware that the first piece of information we receive may not be the most accurate, and we should try to evaluate the situation objectively.

Negotiation and purchases: Anchoring is particularly relevant in negotiations. If one party sets an initial price or figure, that figure can influence the expectations of both parties. For example, if we are buying a house and the initial price is very high, any subsequent offer is likely to seem reasonable by comparison, even if it is still high. In salary negotiations, the first offer can set an anchor that influences the perception of what a fair salary is. To avoid this, it is helpful to come into negotiations with prior research and a clear range of what we consider reasonable, rather than being swayed by the first figure.

<u>Financial decision-making:</u> The anchoring effect can also influence investment decisions or major purchases. Investors can be influenced by the initial purchase price of a stock and make decisions based on that reference rather than objectively assessing the current value of the stock. To counter this bias, it is important to look at the facts independently of the initial price and make decisions based on current information, not on previous anchors.

<u>Marketing and advertising:</u> Anchoring is a common strategy in marketing. Advertisers often display a higher price initially before offering a discount, making the final price appear more attractive in comparison. For example, if a product is originally priced at $100 but is offered for $70, people perceive the price as a good deal because of the higher original price anchor. In everyday life, we need to be aware of these anchoring tactics in advertising and make sure we evaluate the real value of a product or service without being swayed by apparent discounts.

<u>How to make more objective decisions:</u> To avoid falling into the anchoring bias, it is helpful to delay initial judgment and look for more information before making important decisions. It is also important to review figures or data from different angles, asking ourselves if the first information we receive is relevant or is simply influencing our perception. For example, if we

compare prices for a product, we should look at several options rather than relying solely on the first price we see.

<u>Impact on everyday life:</u> In our daily interactions, anchoring can influence how we evaluate the value of objects, services, or even people. First impressions or the initial information we receive can influence how we judge others. Instead of being swayed by first impressions, we should review situations with an open mind and avoid jumping to conclusions.

<u>Life choices and decisions:</u> Anchoring can influence important life decisions, such as choosing a career or a partner. The first information we receive about an option can attract us to that choice, making us less open to other possibilities. To avoid this bias, it is important to consider multiple options and evaluate each one with a balanced approach.

<u>Evaluate emotional investments:</u> In emotional life, anchoring can also influence how we value our relationships. For example, if a relationship starts with a lot of excitement or promise, we may anchor our expectations in that initial phase, even though things change over time. Being aware of this can help us adjust our expectations more realistically and avoid becoming attached to first impressions.

Kahneman and Tversky's anchoring effect demonstrates how our decisions are influenced by the first information we receive, even when that information is irrelevant. In daily life, this bias can affect our decisions in areas such as negotiation, shopping, relationships, and finances. Being aware of anchoring allows us to make more objective decisions and prevent first facts or impressions from disproportionately influencing our choices. To minimize the impact of anchoring, it is crucial to evaluate information from multiple perspectives and question the validity of the initial "anchor."

13. Diffusion of Responsibility Effect

The diffusion of responsibility effect or bystander effect is a psychological phenomenon in which people are less likely to help a victim when others are present. This behavior was identified after the famous Kitty Genovese case, in which a young woman was murdered in New York while many witnesses witnessed the attack, but few did anything to intervene. The effect is based on the idea that in emergencies, the responsibility to act is diffused among those present, leading to inaction.

The Case of Kitty Genovese

In 1964, Kitty Genovese was brutally murdered in a New York neighborhood. Although initial reports indicated that as many as 38 people heard or saw parts of the attack, no one intervened or called the police until it was too late. This case shocked public opinion and led to studies on human behavior in emergencies, culminating in the identification of the bystander effect.

Darley and Latané's experiment on the bystander effect

Following the Kitty Genovese case, psychologists John Darley and Bibb Latané conducted a series of experiments to study how the presence of other people affects someone's willingness to help in an emergency. Their goal was to understand why so many people fail to intervene when others are present.

<u>Participants:</u> Participants were college students who believed they were participating in an experiment

about college life. They were asked to talk about their problems over the intercoms, but they did not see the other participants (who did not exist, except in the experimental group).

Emergency scenario:

During the conversation, a supposed companion (a recording) pretended to suffer an epileptic seizure, desperately requesting help.

Participants believed they were the only witnesses, or that they were accompanied by a small or large group of people.

<u>Results:</u> Darley and Latané found that participants who thought they were alone were much more likely to intervene quickly and seek help. However, as the number of supposed bystanders grew, the likelihood that a participant would act decreased dramatically. When they believed there were others present, many assumed someone else would take responsibility, and therefore took no action.

When participants believed they were alone, approximately 85% acted quickly.

When there was a supposed audience of five people, only 31% intervened.

The diffusion of responsibility effect occurs because when we are in a group, everyone assumes that someone else will take care of the situation. The larger the group, the less likely someone is to intervene, as perceived responsibility is diluted among those present.

Several factors contribute to the effect:

Ambiguity: If the situation is not an emergency, people may wait for cues from others to know if action is needed. This phenomenon is called "social influence," where people look at the behavior of others to determine how they should behave.

Shared responsibility: In a group, each person may feel less direct responsibility to act, as they think someone else will do it.

Fear of making mistakes: Sometimes, people are afraid to intervene in an ambiguous situation for fear of making a mistake or being made to look ridiculous.

Lessons for daily life
Recognizing the bystander effect: Understanding the bystander effect allows us to be more aware of its influence. Knowing that we tend not to act in the presence of others, we can be more attentive and aware when we see a situation that requires help. The next time we see an emergency, we should remember that we cannot assume that someone else will act.

Taking personal responsibility: One of the main lessons of the bystander effect is that we must take responsibility in emergencies, regardless of how many people are around. Often, simple gestures such as calling the police, alerting someone, or asking if everything is okay can make a difference. If everyone assumes that it is their responsibility to act, more people will receive the help they need.

<u>The power of leading by example</u>: If one person acts in an emergency, others are likely to follow suit. Altruistic behavior can be contagious. Being the first to help can encourage others to step in as well. In everyday life, being the first to take the initiative or leading by example can positively influence the people around us.

<u>Applications in daily life and work</u>: The bystander effect can also manifest itself in everyday situations, such as in the workplace. If there is a problem or challenge that no one addresses, everyone may assume that it is "not their responsibility. Instead of waiting for others to take the initiative, taking proactive action can solve problems more quickly and improve the environment in which we operate.

<u>Overcoming social apathy:</u> In a society where people may feel disconnected or indifferent towards others, the bystander effect can be exacerbated. However, being more aware of others and our responsibilities towards them can help counteract this effect. Small acts of kindness, such as helping someone who seems lost or tired, can break the cycle of apathy and make the community stronger.

<u>Developing empathy and active compassion</u>: To combat the bystander effect, it is important to develop active empathy, which involves not only recognizing the needs of others but also acting on them. This skill can improve our interpersonal relationships and foster a sense of community and solidarity. By practicing

active compassion, we can be more willing to step in and help when needed.

<u>Taking control in group situations:</u> In situations where several people witness an emergency, taking the lead can be key. Sometimes, simply pointing at someone directly and telling them to call 911 can solve the problem of diffusing responsibility. Taking control of the situation can prevent group paralysis.

<u>The bystander effect in the digital age:</u> The bystander effect phenomenon has also carried over into the digital world. In situations of online harassment or disinformation campaigns, people may not act or intervene because they assume someone else will. It is crucial to be proactive in digital environments as well, by reporting harmful behavior or supporting those who are victims.

The diffusion of responsibility effect and the case of Kitty Genovese underline the danger of assuming that "someone else" will take care of an emergency. This psychological phenomenon has been demonstrated in numerous studies and has a profound impact on how we act in groups. To combat this effect, it is essential to develop a mindset of personal responsibility, to act proactively, and to be an example for others. By doing so, we not only help those in need but also create a culture of responsibility and mutual care.

14. Intrinsic motivation is more powerful than extrinsic motivation

Intrinsic and extrinsic motivation are two types of motivation that influence human behavior. Intrinsic motivation refers to motivation that comes from within a person, such as the desire to learn or enjoy an activity for its own sake. In contrast, extrinsic motivation refers to external motivations, such as rewards or recognition.

Researchers Edward Deci and Richard Ryan developed the Self-Determination Theory, which holds that intrinsic motivation is more effective and long-lasting than extrinsic motivation. One of their key experiments was designed to explore how external rewards can affect intrinsic motivation.

Deci and Ryan's experiment

Participants: The study involved college students who were incentivized to engage in a series of playful activities, such as puzzle games or similar tasks that required creativity and critical thinking.

Experiment conditions:

Participants were divided into three groups:
- **Group 1** (intrinsic motivation): This group received no external rewards and was allowed to freely participate in the activity.

- **Group 2** (extrinsic motivation): This group was incentivized with monetary rewards for their performance in the activity, which introduced an extrinsic motivation component.

• **Group 3** (unexpected reward): This group received a reward upon completion of the activity but was not informed about it beforehand.

<u>Measuring motivation:</u> After the tasks, the researchers observed how much time participants spent on the activity when they were allowed to choose, without additional rewards or instructions. The goal was to measure the degree to which participants were intrinsically motivated to continue with the activity.

The results showed that:

Group 1, which received no rewards, showed greater interest in continuing the activity and spent more time on it once they were allowed to freely choose.

Group 2, which was incentivized with monetary rewards, showed reduced interest in the activity once the reward was removed. Their motivation decreased, indicating that the external reward had negatively affected their intrinsic motivation.

Group 3, which received an unexpected reward, maintained a similar level of interest to Group 1. This suggests that the unexpected rewards did not harm the participants' intrinsic motivation.

Lessons for daily life
<u>Fostering intrinsic motivation:</u> This study highlights the importance of promoting intrinsic motivation in various areas, such as education and work. People are

more likely to engage and persist in a task when they feel a genuine interest in it. Fostering a love of learning and curiosity can lead to more satisfying and long-lasting outcomes.

<u>Beware of external rewards:</u> External rewards, such as money or recognition, can be effective in the short term, but they can undermine intrinsic motivation in the long term. Instead of relying solely on external incentives, it is important to find ways to motivate people through personal satisfaction and skill development.

<u>Unexpected rewards</u>: Unexpected rewards can be an effective way to reinforce motivation without diminishing intrinsic interest in the task. These types of rewards can be useful in situations where you want to motivate someone without compromising their interest in the activity.

<u>Focus on purpose:</u> Understanding the purpose behind a task or activity can increase intrinsic motivation. Whether in work, education, or personal life, setting meaningful goals and connecting activities to personal values can help increase motivation and engagement.

<u>Cultivate a supportive environment:</u> Creating an environment that supports autonomy, competence, and social relatedness can foster intrinsic motivation. For example, in the classroom, educators can offer students choices about how to approach a task or project, allowing them to feel like they have control over their learning.

<u>Personal development and growth:</u> Intrinsic motivation is critical to personal growth and development. By engaging in activities, we are passionate about, we can improve our skills, expand our knowledge, and find greater satisfaction in our lives.

<u>Recognizing accomplishments:</u> Recognizing and celebrating personal accomplishments, without relying solely on external rewards, can increase intrinsic motivation. Positive feedback and recognition of effort can reinforce the desire to continue moving forward and learning.

<u>Fostering curiosity:</u> In daily life, cultivating curiosity and a desire to learn can lead to greater satisfaction and motivation. Spending time exploring new activities, interests, and passions can help us discover what truly motivates us and pleases us.

Deci and Ryan's studies on intrinsic and extrinsic motivation highlight the importance of motivation that comes from within us. Not only does intrinsic motivation led to greater engagement and satisfaction, but it also fosters deeper, more meaningful learning. By understanding the difference between both types of motivation and their effects on our behavior, we can apply these teachings in our daily lives to promote greater personal well-being and success.

15. Confirmation bias

Confirmation bias is a psychological phenomenon that refers to people's tendency to search for, interpret, and remember information in a way that confirms their preexisting beliefs, while ignoring or downplaying information that might contradict them. This bias can influence how we make decisions and how we process information in everyday life.

One of the most representative studies on confirmation bias was conducted by psychologist Peter Wason in the 1960s.

The Wason Experiment
Card selection task: In this experiment, participants were presented with a task consisting of a set of four cards. Each card had a number on one side and a letter on the other. The cards were:

A (letter)
D (letter)
4 (number)
7 (number)

They were told that if a card had a vowel on one side, then it had an even number on the other side. That is, the rule was: "If there is a vowel, then there is an even number."

Card Selection: Participants were asked to select the cards they would need to flip to determine whether the rule was true. Participants were asked to identify which cards needed to be checked to confirm or refute the rule.

Results: Most participants chose to flip card A (to confirm the rule) and card 4 (also to confirm the rule). However, very few chose to flip card 7, which could provide evidence against the rule, since if there was a vowel on the opposite side, this would prove the rule to be false.

Wason's results showed that participants had a strong tendency to seek out information that confirmed the rule, ignoring the possibility that evidence could refute it. This behavior reflects confirmation bias in action.

Lesson's Lessons for Daily Life

Recognizing confirmation bias: Being aware that we are all prone to this bias can help us question our own beliefs and decisions. It is important to be open to new ideas and information that may challenge our assumptions.

Seek out contrary evidence: In decision-making, it is helpful to actively seek out information that may contradict our beliefs or conclusions. This allows us to gain a more complete view of a situation and make more informed decisions.

Encourage critical thinking: Education in critical thinking can help people become more aware of their own biases and question their beliefs. Encouraging people to examine different perspectives and consider evidence from multiple sources can enrich their understanding of an issue.

Be aware of social media: In the information age, confirmation bias can be amplified by social media, where people tend to follow others who share their opinions and beliefs. This can create echo chambers that reinforce our preconceptions. It is important to diversify the sources of information we consume.

<u>Promote open dialogue</u>: Encouraging open and respectful conversations about controversial topics can help challenge confirmation bias. Listening to the opinions of others and considering their arguments can broaden our understanding and help overcome resistance to information that contradicts our beliefs.

<u>Reflect on past decisions</u>: By reflecting on past decisions, we can identify times when our confirmation bias may have influenced our choices. This reflection exercise can help us become more aware of how bias can affect our behavior in the future.

<u>Foster a learning environment:</u> In educational or work settings, creating an environment that values continuous learning, and constructive criticism can help people overcome confirmation bias. This may involve encouraging students or employees to explore ideas that challenge their usual thinking.

<u>Make informed decisions:</u> Before making important decisions, it is helpful to gather information from a variety of sources and consider different viewpoints. This not only improves the quality of the decision but also helps reduce the risk of falling into confirmation bias.

Confirmation bias is a phenomenon that affects the way we process information and make decisions. The Wason experiment reveals how we tend to seek out and give more weight to information that supports our beliefs while ignoring or downplaying information that might contradict them. By being aware of this bias and applying the lessons in our daily lives, we can improve our ability to make informed decisions and foster stronger critical thinking.

16. The Importance of Self-Care for Mental Health

Self-care is critical to maintaining good mental health, and one of the key studies highlighting the importance of self-care in stress management is the work of psychologist Richard Lazarus. Lazarus is known for his theory of stress and his focus on the cognitive appraisal process that people use to cope with stressful situations.

The Lazarus Study of Stress

Stress Appraisal: Lazarus and his colleague, Susan Folkman, developed the psychological stress theory, which focuses on how people appraise and manage stress. In their research, they conducted a series of studies involving participants experiencing stressful situations, such as work problems, interpersonal relationships, and illness.

Appraisal Process: In his model, Lazarus described two types of appraisals that people conduct when faced with stressful situations:

• Primary appraisal: This involves the initial interpretation of a situation and the assessment of its impact. It asks, "Is this situation dangerous or threatening?"

• Secondary appraisal: This involves the evaluation of the resources and options available to handle the situation. It asks, "What can I do to cope with this situation? Do I have the necessary resources?"

Focus on self-care: In his research, Lazarus emphasized the importance of self-care and the coping strategies that people use to manage stress. He observed that those who implemented self-care techniques, such as mindfulness, physical exercise, and quality time with friends and family, tended to handle stress better and experience fewer mental health problems.

Measuring Outcomes: Researchers measured participants' psychological well-being through surveys and assessments that assessed quality of life, anxiety, depression, and perceived stress. Throughout their studies, it was observed that people who practiced self-care showed greater resilience to stress and better mental health outcomes.

Lessons for daily life

Self-awareness and stress assessment: Understanding how we assess stressful situations is key to effectively managing them. Making a conscious assessment of the situation can help us make informed decisions about how to proceed.

Implementing coping techniques: It is important to develop and practice healthy coping strategies, such as meditation, mindfulness, regular exercise, and time for pleasurable activities. These practices can help reduce anxiety and improve our ability to cope with stress.

Prioritize self-care: Making self-care a priority in our daily lives is critical to maintaining good mental health. This includes taking care of our physical, emotional, and social well-being. Setting aside time for activities we enjoy and that make us feel good can have a positive impact on our mental health.

<u>Seek social support:</u> Lazarus highlighted that having a social support system can be a vital resource for managing stress. Sharing our worries and experiences with friends and family can provide a sense of connection and emotional relief.

<u>Identify and manage stress:</u> Recognizing the sources of stress in our lives and how they affect us is an important first step. By identifying situations that cause us stress, we can take steps to address them and seek effective solutions.

<u>Practice self-empathy:</u> Being compassionate with us and recognizing that it is normal to experience stress and difficulties is essential. Self-empathy can help us healthily address our emotions and avoid negative self-criticism.

<u>Set boundaries:</u> Often, stress comes from over-commitment and a lack of boundaries. Learning to say "no" and setting healthy boundaries in our relationships and responsibilities can contribute to greater mental health and well-being.

<u>Building resilience:</u> Lazarus emphasized that resilience is a capacity that can be developed. Practicing self-care and learning to manage stress effectively can increase our resilience and make us stronger in the face of future challenges.

Richard Lazarus' study of stress highlights the importance of self-care in mental health and how cognitive appraisals affect our perception and management of stress. The lessons learned from his work encourage us to be proactive in our attention to emotional and physical needs and to develop effective strategies for coping with stress. By prioritizing self-care and adopting healthy practices, we can improve our mental health and overall well-being.

17. The Power of Body Language

In the field of social psychology, Dr. Amy Cuddy, a professor and social psychologist at Harvard, conducted a fascinating experiment that highlighted how body language not only affects how others perceive us but also how we perceive ourselves.

Cuddy and her team set out to investigate the concept of "power postures" and how they affect people's self-perception and behavior. The experiment explored the relationship between expansive body postures (called power postures) and the level of confidence and dominance we feel.

Participants: Study participants were asked to adopt one of two postures for two minutes:

• High-power postures: These were expansive, open positions, such as standing with hands on hips or arms outstretched.

• Low-power postures: These were closed, hunched positions, such as crossing arms or leaning forward.

Hormonal measurements: After adopting these postures, researchers measured the levels of two key hormones in the participants:

• Testosterone: Associated with confidence and feelings of power.
• Cortisol: Associated with stress and anxiety.

Results: Participants who adopted the power postures experienced a significant decrease in cortisol levels, indicating a reduction in feelings of stress and anxiety. In contrast, those who adopted low-power postures experienced the opposite effect: their testosterone levels decreased, and their cortisol levels increased, resulting in greater feelings of insecurity and stress.

In addition, in the second part of the experiment, participants were asked to conduct a mock interview for a job, which was assessed by external judges. Those who adopted the high-power postures before the interview were perceived as more confident, charismatic, and having greater leadership ability than those who had adopted low-power postures.

Lessons for daily life
Your posture affects how you feel: One of the most important findings of this experiment is that our posture not only influences how others see us, but how we feel about ourselves. Adopting a power posture, such as standing with your arms akimbo (the "superhero pose"), can boost your confidence in times of self-doubt or stress, such as before a presentation or an interview.

The mind and body are connected: This experiment highlights the deep connection between the body and the mind. Consciously changing our physical posture can alter our brain chemistry and, therefore, our emotional response to challenging situations.

Small changes, big impacts: Simply altering our posture for just two minutes can have a significant impact on how we feel and how we perform in social or professional situations. This finding is particularly helpful for those who face challenges that require confidence, such as public speaking or making important decisions.

<u>Reducing stress through body language:</u> Adopting power postures can be an effective technique for reducing stress and increasing feelings of control. For example, before an important meeting or negotiation, taking a moment to practice a power posture can decrease anxiety and increase feelings of competence.

<u>Improving others' perception of you:</u> Cuddy's research also suggests that body language affects how others perceive us. Adopting open, expansive postures can make you appear more confident and competent to others, improving your relationships and success in social and professional situations.

<u>Postures for critical moments:</u> In situations such as job interviews, important meetings, or even public presentations, practicing a power stance before the event can influence the outcome. The judges who evaluated the interviews in the study observed participants with expansive postures as more charismatic and with greater leadership potential.

Amy Cuddy's experiment reveals that the power of our body language goes beyond simple non-verbal communication; it has a direct impact on our self-perception and emotions. Adopting power poses can not only improve the way others see us, but it can also change how we feel inside. In everyday life, this is a practical and simple tool that we can all use to boost our confidence, reduce stress, and improve our performance in important situations.

18. The Foot-in-the-Door Technique

The foot-in-the-door technique is a persuasion strategy that suggests that people are more likely to agree to a larger request after they have agreed to a small one. This technique was formally investigated in a study by psychologists Jonathan Freedman and Scott Fraser in 1966, who demonstrated how small initial compromises can lead to larger concessions later.

Description of the experiment
Purpose of the study: Freedman and Fraser wanted to test the hypothesis that people are more likely to agree to a large request if they have previously agreed to a smaller, easier-to-fulfill request. To investigate this, they experimented with residents in suburban neighborhoods in California.

In the first part of the study, the researchers approached a group of residents and made a small request: to put up a very small sign in their window or yard that supported road safety. Most people agreed to this request, as it was a simple and unintrusive request.

In the second part of the study, weeks later, the same researchers approached those people and asked them for a much larger favor: to put up a large sign in their yards that said, "Drive Safely," which was a much more intrusive and visible request.

Results:

Residents who had agreed to the first small request (putting up the small sign) were much more likely to agree to the second larger request (the larger sign) compared to those who had only been asked for the large request directly, without having agreed to the first smaller request.

Approximately 76% of people who had agreed to the first small request agreed to the second larger request. In contrast, only 17% of people who were asked directly for the large sign agreed to the request.

This study introduced the concept of the foot-in-the-door technique, which is based on the idea that once people have said "yes" to a small request, they are more likely to agree to larger requests due to several psychological factors:

Consistency: People tend to want to be consistent with their previous decisions. If they have already agreed to a small favor, they are likely to continue saying "yes" to related requests to maintain consistency in their behavior.

Commitment: Agreeing to an initial small request creates a sense of commitment. Once committed, people often feel an obligation to comply with larger requests that reinforce that initial commitment.

Lessons for daily life
Gradual persuasion: The foot-in-the-door technique is useful when we want to convince someone to do something significant. If we start by asking for a small favor or commitment, it will be easier to get them to agree to a larger request in the future. This can be valuable in situations such as sales, negotiations, or even in personal relationships.

Use in social relationships: When we are trying to influence the behavior of others, it is more effective to start with small requests. For example, if you want a friend or colleague to help you with an important project, asking them for something minor at first (such as an opinion or advice) can make them more willing to get more deeply involved later.

Application at work: Leaders or managers who are looking for their employees to take on greater responsibilities can start with small tasks. As employees become committed to these tasks, they will be more likely to take on larger, more meaningful tasks without feeling like they are being asked for too much.

Building habits: This technique can also be applied to you. If you want to acquire a new habit or make a significant change in your life, start with a small commitment. For example, if your goal is to start exercising, committing yourself to just five minutes of exercise a day can be a good first step to eventually taking on a more intense and lasting routine.

Avoiding abrupt rejection: Asking for too much right from the start can lead to resistance or rejection. The foot-in-the-door technique teaches that it is more effective to gradually increase requests, which decreases the likelihood of an abrupt refusal.

Building trust in sales or marketing: In the commercial realm, companies can use this technique by offering free or low-cost products or services to attract customers. Once customers have taken the first step, they will be more inclined to accept more expensive or committed offers.

<u>Changing social behavior:</u> If you are looking to influence a behavior change, such as encouraging pro-environmental or safety attitudes, starting with small steps is key. By getting people to engage in minimal ways at first, it's easier for them to adopt more substantial behaviors in the long run.

Freedman and Fraser's study of the foot-in-the-door technique demonstrates how small initial commitments can pave the way for larger requests. In everyday life, this technique has multiple applications, from persuasion in sales and negotiations to creating new personal habits. Understanding and applying this technique allows us to more effectively influence others and, in turn, build commitments that help us achieve our own goals.

19. The Zeigarnik Effect

The Zeigarnik Effect is a psychological phenomenon discovered by Soviet psychologist Bluma Zeigarnik in 1927. This effect refers to people's tendency to remember unfinished or interrupted tasks better than completed tasks. Zeigarnik observed that when an activity is interrupted, it creates a kind of mental tension that causes it to remain in our memory until it is completed.

Description of the experiment Zeigarnik began his investigation after noticing something curious at a restaurant. I have observed that waiters could remember tables' orders if they were not paid, but as soon as the bills were settled, they quickly forgot the details of those orders. This sparked his interest in studying how people remember complete and incomplete tasks.

Zeigarnik gathered a group of participants and asked them to perform a series of simple tasks, such as solving puzzles or completing manual exercises.

Some of the participants were allowed to complete the tasks, while others were interrupted before they could finish them.

After a while, Zeigarnik asked the participants to recall the tasks they had completed.

Zeigarnik found that participants were significantly better at remembering tasks they had failed to complete, compared to tasks they had finished.

This finding showed that people have a natural tendency to keep unfinished tasks more present in their memory, due to a "cognitive tension" that seeks resolution.

Lessons for daily life

<u>Motivation to complete tasks:</u> The Zeigarnik effect can be used as a source of motivation to complete projects or tasks. When we leave something unfinished, our mind keeps reminding us to finish it, which can create psychological discomfort that drives us to act. Positively using this discomfort can help prevent procrastination.

<u>Planning work and study:</u> By interrupting briefly while working or studying, you can take advantage of the Zeigarnik effect to keep information fresh in your mind. For example, if you're studying for an exam, taking regular breaks while studying can help you retain what you've learned better.

<u>Productivity techniques:</u> The Zeigarnik effect is behind many productivity techniques that suggest starting with small tasks and leaving them partially unfinished. For example, in the Pomodoro technique, you work for some time and then take a break. Failing to complete the task in its entirety can increase the desire to return to it and complete it later, helping to maintain focus.

<u>Anxiety reduction:</u> In situations where people have multiple tasks on their plate, the Zeigarnik effect can increase feelings of stress or anxiety, as uncompleted tasks tend to stay in the mind. Being aware of this effect can help us manage better our to-do list, prioritizing those that generate the most mental stress.

Marketing and entertainment: The Zeigarnik effect is frequently used in marketing and the media. For example, in television series, episodes often end on cliffhangers, or unresolved tension points, which creates a need in the viewer to watch the next episode. Brands also use this effect in advertising, creating campaigns that leave the consumer with a feeling of incompleteness, which motivates them to learn more or make a purchase.

Improving memory: One way to take advantage of the Zeigarnik effect to improve memory is to chunk the tasks or information we are learning. Voluntarily interrupting an activity, the mind will keep it more active in our memory, which can help us remember important details better.

Managing stress at work: Being aware of the Zeigarnik effect can help us be more compassionate with ourselves when we feel like we can't switch off from our unfinished tasks. This cognitive tension is natural, and we can use it to get better organized, prioritizing those tasks that take up more mental space.

The Zeigarnik effect reveals how our mind prioritizes unfinished tasks, which creates a "mental tension" that drives us to finish them. This phenomenon is extremely useful for improving our motivation, productivity, and information retention. Understanding and applying this principle in daily life allows us to better manage our pending tasks, avoid procrastination, and stay focused on achieving our goals, both professionally and personally.

20. The Yerkes-Dodson law

The Yerkes-Dodson law is a psychological principle that relates the level of arousal (activation or excitation) to performance. This law states that there is a curve-shaped relationship between arousal and performance: at low or very high levels of arousal, performance is poor; while at an intermediate level of arousal, performance is optimal. It was discovered in 1908 by psychologists Robert M. Yerkes and John D. Dodson.

Description of the experiment

Purpose of the study: Yerkes and Dodson wanted to explore how the difficulty of a task and the levels of stimulation affected subjects' performance in performing tasks. In their experiment, they worked with mice to observe how they responded to different levels of stimulus (electricity) in a discrimination task.

The mice were taught to choose between two doors, one of which was associated with a reward, while the other door provided a mild electric shock.

The researchers varied the intensity of the electric shock (which functioned as a stressor or motivation) to see how it affected the mice's ability to learn and perform the task correctly.

They also varied the difficulty of the task, making the doors distinguishable, which made the discrimination task harder or easier.

The mice performed best when the intensity of the shock (the level of stress or motivation) was moderate.

If the shock was too mild, the mice were not sufficiently motivated to perform the task; if the shock was too strong, they became distracted or confused, which prevented them from learning properly.

The conclusion was that optimal performance was achieved at an intermediate level of arousal or stress. Too little or too much of this factor impaired performance.

Conclusion of the study: The Yerkes-Dodson law postulates that performance increases with physiological or mental arousal, but only up to a certain point. After that point, when the arousal becomes too high, performance begins to decrease.

Lessons for everyday life
Find the sweet spot: Research shows that a certain degree of stress or arousal is necessary to maximize task performance. For example, in work or study situations, a small degree of pressure (such as a deadline or the expectation to perform well) can improve focus and motivation. However, too much stress can lead to mental block, anxiety, and burnout.

Stress management: The Yerkes-Dodson law suggests that not all stress is negative. Learning to manage your arousal level is key to optimizing performance. If you feel too relaxed, it might be helpful to set clear goals or deadlines to increase motivation. If, on the other hand, you are too stressed, techniques such as meditation, deep breathing, or rest can help reduce excess pressure.

<u>Adjust the difficulty level of tasks:</u> The relationship between arousal and performance also depends on the difficulty of the task. For simple tasks, higher levels of activation can be beneficial, but for complex tasks that require concentration, a moderate level of stress is more helpful. In everyday life, this means that when you are faced with a difficult task, it is best to be calm and focused, while for easier tasks, a little more pressure can help you get them done quickly.

<u>Motivation and productivity:</u> If you are too relaxed, you could lose motivation to complete your goals. Applying some pressure to yourself, such as setting specific goals or making a public commitment, can increase the level of activation and improve your productivity. However, it is essential not to overexert yourself, as too much pressure could lead to ineffectiveness.

<u>Performance in high-pressure situations:</u> The Yerkes-Dodson law is particularly relevant in high-performance situations, such as exams, job interviews, or sporting events. These are times when it is crucial to reach an optimal level of activation. Too much relaxation can lead to apathy, while too much nervousness can cause mistakes. Controlling your arousal level before these events is essential to achieving good performance.

<u>Motivation in teamwork:</u> In work environments, the Yerkes-Dodson law can help leaders understand the importance of adjusting the level of pressure based on the tasks and the team's capacity. Applying too much pressure to a complicated project could create anxiety and affect performance, while too little pressure could cause team members to lose focus.

In daily life, we can leverage this law to improve our performance in a variety of areas. If you need to complete a task you've been putting off, increasing the pressure or sense of urgency a little could be beneficial. On the other hand, if you're feeling overwhelmed, taking a moment to relax could allow you to get back to the task with greater clarity and efficiency.

The Yerkes-Dodson law offers valuable insight into how arousal or stress influences performance. The balance between too little and too much stress is crucial to achieving peak performance. Applying this law in daily life helps us manage stress, improve productivity, and tackle challenging tasks efficiently. The key is to find that middle ground that motivates us without overwhelming us.

———————†———————